Quiet Gardens

by William Claassen

Books

Alone in Community:
Journeys into Monastic Life Around the World

Another World: A Retreat in the Ozarks

Journey Man: A World Calling

Play

Quiet Gardens

Quiet Gardens

William Claassen

Cornel & Williams
Columbia, Missouri

Quiet Gardens is published by Cornel & Williams, PO Box 535, Columbia, Missouri 65205, CornelWilliams48@yahoo.com, (573)449-8764.

Publisher's Cataloging-in-Publication Data

Claassen, William, 1948-
  Quiet Gardens/William Claassen
  p. cm.
  ISBN 978-0-692-28000-3
1. Hallucinogenic drugs and religious experience -Drama. 2. Spirituality -Drama. 3. Friendship -Drama. 4. Oregon -Drama. I. Title.

PS3603.L333 Qu54 2014
813.6 -dc23   2014915866

first printing: November 2014
printed by CreateSpace

Cover and Interior Design: Alyssa Blevins

to Silent Meetings

The foundation for *Quiet Gardens* was a tape recording of an event that occurred in 1985. The participants were Steve Podry, his former wife; Lucy Banks, and myself. With the permission from Lucy and me, Steve recorded the event. He later transcribed it, word for word, in play form.

For more than two decades, Steve and I revisited the transcription dozens of times. We edited and re-edited the material with the intention of creating a one act play.

At a certain point in our process, it became clear that Steve and I had two very different visions as to how to expand and mold the work into a one act. Because of our major differences, he suggested that we write two separate plays.

Initially, I didn't think it was a good idea. Eventually, I realized that's what we needed to do.

Quiet Gardens was written in collaboration with Peter Beiger, Lisa Lapp, and Steve Podry. I want to thank them for their advice, edits, and revisions. And a special acknowledgement to Lucy Banks, Daria Barretta, Robert Claassen, Dave Collins, Steve Gallagher, Rocket Kirchner, and the Hugh Stephens Library staff.

The first reading of *Quiet Gardens* was staged in the A.P. Green Chapel, at the University of Missouri in Columbia, on August 23, 2014. The reading was produced and directed by William Claassen. The cast was as follows:

Neil .... Dave Collins

Ginny .... Daria Barretta

Thad .... Steve Gallagher

Characters

Neil
Ginny
Thad

Time and Setting

Eventide, October 1985.
Eugene, Oregon.

Place

The action takes place in the front room of a two bedroom cottage. When the lights come up, we see an upright piano and bench against the side wall stage left. Upstage from the piano is a wide, arched entranceway into the small kitchen. Downstage left is a flat top desk and chair covered with books, papers, and a reel to reel tape recorder. In the back wall are two doors that lead into Thad and Ginny's bedroom and the guest room. Between the doors are book cases filled with Thad's collection of hand written daily journals, spanning more than a decade, and an assortment of books. Downstage right corner is a wood burning stove. In the center of the room sits an easy chair and a comfortable couch with a small table and lamp placed between them. A coffee table sits nearby.

The audience hears muffled voices and the clanking of pans and dishes coming from the kitchen. They can see Neil and Thad washing and drying the dinner dishes and putting them away. Within the past hour, the men have eaten magical (psilocybin) mushrooms during their departure ritual for Neil. They are just beginning to feel the effects. Months ago, the men harvested the mushrooms from a nearby forest with this particular evening in mind. Although they have experienced altered states of mind in the past, this is their introduction to magical mushrooms.

Neil, in his mid-30s, is wearing loose fitting khakis and a faded, blue, cotton work shirt. Originally, he came to Oregon to join a tree planting cooperative. A native of small town Kansas, Neil is single, perpetually restless and a world traveler. After working two years as a trial assistant for a Portland law firm, he has decided to move to Pennsylvania to join an intentional spiritual community. On his trip east, he is passing through Eugene to spend a few days with his close friends, Thad and Ginny.

From St. Louis, Thad is in his late 20s. Lean and rangy, he wears wire rimmed glasses and faded blue jeans with a green, plaid, flannel shirt. After teaching high school English for a number of years in his home town, Thad decided to head for Oregon on a cross country bicycle trek and settled in Eugene. He is a disciplined daily journal writer, a musician and a poet who is currently pursuing a graduate degree in counseling.

Thad is the intellectual of the three and frequently self-absorbed.

The two men became close friends when they rented individual rooms in a nearby boarding house before Neil moved to Portland to work for the law firm. Both have a keen interest in music, ritual and spirituality. They also have an abiding hunger for capturing a *sense of awe* in their respective lives. *Pushing the envelope* is a habit they have in common.

Ginny, curled up on the front room couch and working on a *NY Times* crossword puzzle, was born and raised in the borough of Manhattan. She is Thad's wife of two months. Still speaking with a slight New York accent, Ginny thinks of herself as a bohemian. Seven years older than her husband, she came to Oregon a decade ago to visit a friend and never left. With a fair complexion, dark, shoulder length hair and a full figure, Ginny is dressed in a colorful peasant skirt and a puffy white blouse. An independent woman who is clearly mystified and, at times, perplexed by her new spouse, she is a fulltime nurse and presently on call at the local hospital. Because of her job responsibilities, she has not eaten any of the mushrooms. Ginny is the most practical of the three.

The three friends are energetic, playful and thoroughly enjoying one another's company. They are also feeling a bit anxious about this new adventure.

Ginny

(Calls out to Neil and Thad in the kitchen.) What begins with a **Z**, ends with a **C**, causes fermentation and has nine letters?

Neil

(Pause.) Repeat your question, por favor. *(Chuckles.)*

Thad

(Laughing.) And please repeat it slowly.

Ginny

Okay, listen up! *(Slowly.)* What begins with a **Z**, ends with a **C**, causes fermentation and has nine letters?

Neil

(Pause.) Begins with a **Z**, huh? *(Laughing.)*

Ginny

That's right and ends with a **C** like in **can't** get it.

Thad

(Laughing.) How many letters?

Ginny

Nine.

Neil

(Razzing Ginny.) What was the definition again?

Ginny

To cause fermentation. *(Plays along.)*

Neil

(Pause.) Golly, it's just right on the tip of my tongue.

Thad

Yeah, it's on the tip of my tongue, too. *(Laughing.)*

Neil

And it ends with a **C** like in **can't** get it, huh?

Ginny

Never mind, fellas. *(Smiles big.)* I can tell those magical mushrooms have already started to kick in. *(Pause.)*

Neil

(Enters the front room and plops down in the easy chair.) Took a while but we finally finished the dishes.

Ginny

(Looks up from her puzzle.) Glad you boys were capable of completing the task at hand. *(Tentatively returns to her puzzle.)*

Thad

(Enters the front room, saunters over to the desk, turns on the reel to reel tape recorder and sits down on the piano bench facing the other two.) Wow! *(Swings around and plays a simple, slow melody with his right hand.)*

Neil

There was no sense of this kind of experience when we were chewing on those mushrooms.

Thad

You can't get it. *(Continues to play the simple melody.)*

Neil

No, you can't. *(Pause.)* You know that Buddhist retreat ... that silent meditation I went to?

Thad

(Stops playing. Turns back around.) Oh, yeah.

Neil

After being silent for days and days ... and then breaking the silence?

Thad

Yeah.

Neil

(Becomes more animated as he talks.) I didn't wanna do it! So I kept putting it off. Hour after hour, I put it off. I walked away from breaking my silence and went on a long hike in the woods. I felt so totally comfortable in silence. When other people were just ... were just like climbing the walls to communicate, I felt more and more ... and more and more comfortable!

Thad

Like you didn't ever want to let the silence go?

Neil

Right! Right! Like that was the only way I wanted to relate to the others. Because ... there's ... Why not?

Thad

(Laughing.) Right on, brother!

Neil

I mean we were all doing it; relating through the silence. And nobody had to be told what our name was, what we had accomplished, where we had travelled or...

Ginny

(Sits up.) So, going through that standard routine? *(Lays down the crossword puzzle on the small table.)*

Neil

(Nods his head and continues.) or even use those terms, you know, to define who we were. It was all coming from gestures and feelings. There was some physical contact, but minimal ... and eye contact and looks and just getting comfortable with who

we were. You know, words don't express ... *(Frustrated.)* Arrgh! *(Thad and Ginny chuckle.)* It's just people being themselves ... or me being myself. You know? *(Throws up his hands.)* Oh, I don't know!

Thad

No. Right. You didn't want to lose that.

Neil

I didn't want to lose ... I didn't want to have to go back and ... a ... a ... and lose that basic way of communicating to other people and picking that up from me to them to whatever. *(All laugh.)*

Thad

And so ...

Neil

And so it's like, it's like ... such a relief for people to talk. Not all people. That's not true though. There were some people who felt the same way as I did and other ... Oh God, it's a conundrum! *(All laugh.)*

Ginny

I would be like ... terribly confused.

Neil

(Completes his thought.) So, at the end of the retreat most people jumped on it. Jumped on it and just started talking immediately; enjoying one another's company.

Ginny

I would do that for sure. *(Chuckles.)*

Neil

And some people maybe, like, took an hour. And then a few others took an hour and a half. That was an interesting process to watch, to say the least, although I didn't stick around to watch it. *(Laughs at himself.)* But ... anyway ... *(Pause.)* Do you understand me; what I'm saying?

Ginny

Mmm ... yeah, I do.

Thad

(Seated at the piano with head down and eyes closed.) I'm with you. *(Swings around and plays up an octave scale.)*

Neil

Okay.

Thad

It's just ... It's just sending me to other places, too. *(Plays same scale down an octave then swings back around and faces the other two.)* But it's not like ... not apart from it.

Neil

I just wanted to sort of check ... both places and see if you all ... could ...

Ginny

Oh yeah. I understood it exactly! *(Reaches out to support him.)* But I understood it through the words, you know, not the feelings, which is funny 'cause I wouldn't feel that way ordinarily.

Neil

Right, no, I know. That's what you just said. You'd be the one talking the talk. *(Chuckles.)* You said you'd be that kind of person.

Ginny

Right, right. So, the only way I understood was through words.

Neil

Right. Yeah. *(Pause.)* No, I don't get that! No … you said when
I said … *(Looks around confused. Ginny is laughing.)*

*(Thad chokes with laughter then swings back around and plays a simple
boogie woogie melody with his right hand.)*

Neil

(Laughing.) This is just going back and forth. When I said there
were some people who jumped on the words immediately, you
said, "That's what I would do." That's what you're talking about?

Ginny

Right.

Neil

I can understand that.

(Thad plays the boogie woogie melody briefly.)

Ginny

I know but what I'm saying is I can even understand your experi-
encing silence; of enjoying no words through your words.

Neil

Oh! Great, great …

Ginny

But … so … it's the words I can understand not necessarily the feelings, see?

Neil

Yeah, I see. *(Finally gets it.)* That's right.

Ginny

So, that's why I need words. *(Smiles big.)*

Neil

Yeah. *(Chuckles.)* Okay, I got it. *(Stands, pumps his arms up and down and chants.)* I got it! I got it! I got it … *(Ginny and Thad stand and join him in the arm pumping and the chanting for a moment.)* Great! And I don't like them for that same reason. *(All three plop down on the couch. Pause.)*

Ginny

But without them I wouldn't understand.

Neil

Ohhhh, yes you would. Yes you would.

Ginny

I would understand some feelings without words but not feelings I would necessarily want to share.

Neil

True, that may be true. *(Pause.)*

Thad

(As if making an announcement.) It's both sides!

Neil

I know.

Thad

(Gets up and returns to the piano.) Both sides are true!

Neil

Okay, that's right.

Ginny

(Playfully.) Right on, Thad!

Thad

See, both sides are true! *(Addresses Neil as if he still doesn't get it.)*

Neil

(Suddenly agitated, edgy and feeling vulnerable.) Okay! Both sides are true! *(Clearly shaken up and surprised by his reaction, Neil jumps up and strides into the kitchen. Ginny looks puzzled.)*

Thad

Hmm. *(Plays chords reminiscent of a dirge.)*

Neil

(Takes a moment to recover then calls out.) My water's burning! *(Piano playing stops. Neil re-enters the front room speaking with a British accent.)* We're serving tea and biscuits now. Anybody care for a spot a tea and a biscuit?

Ginny

(Replies with a similar accent.) Oh yes, jolly good. I would simply love some. Thank you, old chum

Thad

(No accent.) I'm doing j-u-s-t fine. *(Returns to playing the dirge-like chords.)*

Neil

Right-O then. *(Begins to go back into the kitchen but stops near the piano. Drops the accent.)* Can you play something other than that on the piano, p-l-e-a-s-e?

Thad

But it'll totally change time and space. Understand?

Neil

That's okay. Let it change. But just put it in a different mode for now, please. *(Thad plays a repetitive series of notes in the Philip Glass style. Neil chuckles and moves back into the kitchen.)* The funny thing is, as I'm making tea, is that often times I ... uh... uh ... *(Laughs at himself for losing his thought, walks back into the front room with two mugs of tea and cookies and stops at the piano.)* You're just sitting and listening to one note flip over into the other.

Thad

All of it, yeah.

Neil

(Walks to the couch, places mugs and cookies on the coffee table, sits by Ginny and snuggles.) As I was saying, the funny thing is that ...

Thad

(Stops playing. Has a private revelation.) Wow!

Neil

I don't know. I forgot what I was gonna say, again!

Thad

We have to do the best we can, man. We do what we can. *(All three burst into laughter. Thad and Neil jump up and high five. Ginny stands and joins the men in a group hug.)*

Neil

(While standing, they open up their circle and hold hands.) The reason I have such a good time with you folks ... I catch elements of this unspoken state ... being with you two in the straight world, you know, so to speak? *(Pause. Addresses Thad.)* Are we high or what?

Thad

Oh yeah!

Neil

And there are only a couple of other people in my life where I can feel this way. *(Pause. They break apart and Thad sits down in the easy chair. Neil and Ginny return to the couch.)*

Ginny

(Speaks to Thad. He's looking down at the floor again with eyes closed.) Even though you and I are so different, that's one thing we have in common and I love you for that. *(She gets up and kisses the top of his head.)*

Neil

Bravo! Bravo! *(Applauds.)*

Thad

(Looks up.) You're talking to me?

Ginny

Of course!

Thad

Oh! *(Ginny kisses him on the lips.)*

Neil

It's like even when we aren't, we are. You know?

Ginny

Right you are! *(Pause.)* 'Scuse me you two crazy guys. I have to call the hospital and check in. *(Begins to exit into the bedroom but swings back around.)* Easy boys! *(Pulls the door shut behind her.)*

Thad

(Long pause.) I was thinking, you turn on the tape recorder but there's nothing to say. You can't put it into words.

Neil

Well, I don't know if going back and listening … *(Pause.)* No, actually you would. *(Gets up, walks over to the desk and sits down next to the tape recorder.)* I think you would understand what's being said. Because there's that element, even without the shrooms, that I think …

Thad

What I mean is the tape recorder needs words.

Neil

(Gestures towards the recorder.) Well, what are we doing? *(Stands and begins to do slow, improvisational movement around the room.)*

Thad

Right, okay, that's part of it. *(Jumps up, joins Neil in the movement and they begin to do contact improvisation with one another.)* But … but when we're inside our many worlds, the tape … the tape recorder can't bring that inside.

Neil

(Continue the contact improvisation as they talk.) No, that's true. It's like listening to Timothy Leary tripping off on a record or something. *(Pause.)* But … except if you've been there before. I mean, it may make some sense.

Thad

And we are there.

Neil

(Laughing.) And we are there! *(They stop moving and embrace fully. Pause. Loosen the embrace and continue the contact improvisation.)* But, I mean, you're not gonna use that tape to make a record to distribute to thousands of people out there.

Thad

That's true. We're just going to laugh about it.

Neil

We're gonna laugh. And, you're gonna listen to it and Ginny's gonna listen. And maybe I'll listen to it again in the future and still, I think, understand it. *(They laugh and embrace again. Ginny walks out of the bedroom, joins the hug then heads for the kitchen.)*

Thad

Everything okay?

Ginny

(Stops and turns around to answer.) Yeah. Everything okay with you?

Thad

You bet. *(Pause.)* Gin, may I have a glass of orange juice, please?

Ginny

Anything for you, sweetheart.

Thad

(Ginny walks into the kitchen. Thad sits down in the easy chair and Neil plops down on the couch. Pause.) See, when I was tripping a few years ago, I wrote it all down. I wrote and wrote and wrote and wrote and wrote. But it still didn't quite do it!

Neil

Didn't do what?

Thad

It didn't say it. It didn't put it all into words. So, there's all these different ways of like ... the tape recorder and ... uh ... trying to write it down and it just keeps happening. *(Pause. Abruptly and loudly changes the subject.)* Can we agree on change?

Neil

(Pause.) Wow! *(Surprised at Thad's volume and abrupt change of topic.)* What?

Thad

Let's agree on change; that change is happening.

Neil

Oh ... yeah, sure.

Thad

That's what it all comes down to. And it erases everything then, too.

Neil

Right, Thad. Right. *(Puts hand on Thad's knee to show support.)*

Thad

But it also stays the same.

Neil

Well, I'm not so sure that it stays …

(Ginny comes back into the room, hands Thad a glass of orange juice and sits down on the couch.)

Thad

Thanks. *(Realizes that Neil was interrupted.)* What were you saying?

Neil

Does it stay the same? If you really believe in the idea of change; that things are constantly changing, then things are constantly changing! They don't come back to … You know, there are elements of … *(Thad's laughter interrupts Neil's convoluted comment.)* I'm gonna keep on goin' with this. Okay?

Thad

That's it! That's the point. That's what I'm trying to get to. Keep it up.

Neil

Okay, there are these elements. Okay? *(Jumps up and paces the floor as he shares his thoughts.)*

Thad

Yeah.

Neil

There are these elements that stay the same that we know of and are familiar with and so we hold on to them along the way. But change keeps happenin'. I mean like it can be my grandfather's old Navajo rug I hold on to.

Thad

(Jumps up and begins pacing the floor, too.) See, it's not the words. It's the performance in the moment. I mean we're performing the reality that we're feeling ...

Neil

Yes! That's it! That's right, Thad baby.

Thad

(Continues with thought.) that we're living or that the words ...

Neil

... somehow connect.

Ginny

(Stands.) That's true, for sure.

All

(Move around and chant.) True, true, true ...

Neil

Because I think that's part of it.

Ginny

That's all that'll be left on that tape ... words!

Neil

Ah, right!

All

(Move and chant.) Right, right, right ...

Ginny

And that's fine. That's fine!

All

(Move and chant.) Fine, fine, fine ... *(They stop, join in a group hug and move back to the couch.)*

Neil

(To Ginny.) See, now you're bringing our attention back to ... to ... Ah hell, I can't remember. That's okay. I don't care.

Thad

It's all part of the shift!

Neil

(Remembers. Jumps up and starts pacing again.) Oh, oh, the Navajo rug! So, the point is, I go through all these changes but I hold on to that Navajo rug. *(Thad teases Neil with laughter.)* Right?

Ginny

That's right. That's right.

Neil

(Slows down.) Because that's something I know from the past that I like and that ... *(Shakes his head.)* that just roots me

somewhere, you see, as I continually go through one change after another, after another, after another, *(Pause. Unexpectedly on the
verge of tears.)* after another, after another.

Ginny

You're right. You're right. *(Reassures and comforts him.)*

Neil

(Laughs and cries at the same time.) And I'll pick up other things
along the way, too. *(Sits down at the desk.)* I mean we all do that.

Thad

That's right, brother! That's right.

Neil

(Recovers.) But see, the change goes on! I mean, it's like you may
continue wearing that damn plaid shirt, Thad, right? *(Pause.)* And
you'll wear that damn plaid shirt for years but that doesn't mean
… *(Both men are laughing.)* that doesn't mean you're not changing
every day. Right?

Thad

(Razzing Neil.) I take a shower and change my clothes every day,
buddy.

Neil

I mean, we really are changing all the time! But nobody wants to admit it. You know? Nobody wants to say that they're changing, all the time, because that's the flip-side. *(Pause.)* See, that's when it becomes like fear or whatever's on that flip-side.

Ginny

I'm always interested in that flip-side ... in the other dimension; the opposition.

Neil

You are?

Ginny

Yeah! I like that side.

Neil

Which side, the fear side?

Ginny

Yeah! What I mean is that's the tunnel back to this world.

Thad

(Pause.) You're right, Gin. That's the tunnel back to this world. Right on! *(Pause.)* Ginny, I'm glad you're here. This is the best way of recording it; have a witness. *(Ginny kisses him on the cheek.)*

Neil

Right! Right. See, right now, I hesitate to go to that fear side because … *(Emotions begin to well up again.)* because you know as an explorer you can get lost in your head. *(The conversation triggers a reminder of his nervous breakdown a few years ago. He's suddenly feeling vulnerable and wants to avoid talking about that experience.)* But that's where you would go to, isn't it Thad?

Thad

(Chuckling.) I … I can't follow you right now. I'm seeing and thinking in holograms. *(Feels anxious.)* Start talking again.

Neil

Oh, okay. I'll just keep on talkin' then. *(Moves back to the couch.)*

Ginny

(Guides the tripsters.) Keep talking to him, Neil.

Neil

So, I would see you looking at that flip-side, Thad, and being very interested in that fear side … *(Supports Thad.)* and exploring that fear. I mean, that would be your interest and you could go there right now.

Thad

You mean in this moment … here and now?

Neil

No, no, no, no, no, not the here and now, Thad. I mean just generally; your work with counseling, etc., etc. I mean that's … that's important. *(Looks at Thad and Ginny.)* Are you with me?

Thad

Please keep going, man. I'm with you. *(Supports Neil.)*

Ginny

I am, too.

Neil

All right, and that's not where I'm at right now. It's like I won't ignore that and I acknowledge it. But right now, I'm not in a head space to go back into another role as an explorer. You see, folks?

Thad

Yeah, yeah.

Ginny

Sure Neil, I totally understand.

Neil

Although that's very important … and … and at some point exploring will happen; will happen for all of us again. Ya know?

Thad

(Pause.) Well, it is happening right now, too. *(They laugh.)* I mean here we are playing explorers! You see? It's great! *(Slowly slides down from the couch onto the floor.)*

Neil

(Revelation.) You are right. You are a-b-s-o-l-u-t-e-l-y right!

Thad

(Amazed.) `Cause I followed them; all the words that you said. I followed them, Neil. And then …

Pay attention to how your thoughts flow at different times of the day and do your best to optimize your creativity and productivity around these natural cycles.

I find that some tasks can be accomplished with ease and effortlessness at certain phases of the day that correspond to our quieter mind states. These tasks would otherwise be much more challenging to complete, especially sigmas and omegas which require high-level strategic clarity. Use this to your advantage. Sequence your tasks in alignment with this observation.

9. The Profound Value of a Quiet Mind

All this work on life systems will be dramatically improved if you, in parallel, can move towards a quieter mind.

The noise and speed of the world, the siren call of social media, judgment, and spiteful opinions will cloud your mind. They will influence your brain waves to become distressed and you will not be able to see the truth of your own personal path or the truth of this world.

To be super effective with this work, it is best to live at the bottom of the ocean as much as possible in our minds. We should strive to live below the tumultuous waves of random thoughts, societal influence, our fears, and concerns.

All these pieces have a place but our work does depend on optimizing the brain waves that produce our best ideas, outputs, and health outcomes. These spring from the quiet, slow, and timeless center of ourselves.

I highly recommend integrating some type of practice that helps you quiet your mind into your life system.

Neil

It's okay. *(Slides down to the floor beside Thad.)*

Thad

And then …

Ginny

And then what? *(Slides down to the floor on the other side of Thad.)*

Thad

And then I could see what I did. I was performing the exact words that you were describing.

Neil

Yeah? Okay. So, I mean, what does that have anything to do with …

Thad

I can't remember. *(All laugh.)*

Ginny

Then are we making a judgment about it?

Thad

(Pounds his fist on the floor.) No, not at all! No, no, no!

Neil

Okay, okay. You're just relating the experience. Is that what you're doing? *(Confused. Tries to calm Thad down.)*

Thad

(Gathers himself.) Wait a minute. Wait a minute.

Neil

We were just talking. You're just talking.

Thad

(Makes the same point once again.) It keeps coming back to performing! *(Pause.)* As soon as ... as soon as ... whatever you were describing. I can't remember what you were describing, Neil.

Neil

What was I describing? *(Jumps up and begins to pace around the room again.)* Oh ... your shirt ... your damn plaid shirt? Or, was I describing my grandfather's Navajo rug? Or, I was describing the ... oh, oh, oh ... explorer!

Ginny

Right, the explorer! *(Moves back up to the couch.)*

Neil

You were the explorer going back; going into that flip-side of fear. *(Walks back to the couch.)*

Thad

Right! *(Moves back up to the couch.)* Then my response to it, I was doing the exact ...

Neil

(Jumps in.) You were watching yourself do it?

Thad

No, not exactly, although that too. *(All laughing.)* You know ... there's room for all of it.

Neil

Yeah, I know. But I didn't know if you were setting up the

scene or actually in the scene. We were just tripping. *(Long pause. All three try to catch up with the conversational thread.)*

Thad

It comes back to basics like ... *(Has another private revelation.)* Wow! *(Pause.)*

(Ginny gets up and walks into the kitchen with her tea mug. Neil follows with mug in hand. We hear them bantering in the kitchen with their British accents. They playfully clink spoons against mugs. Thad remains on the couch clearly in awe of something.)

Neil

This mug is mine and I was going to have a spot of cream.

Ginny

Oh, I put it back in the fridge, old chum.

Neil

Jolly good, then. Let me get it.

Ginny

No, no, no, I'll get it for you, old chum.

Neil

No, no, dearie, I've got it. By jove, I've got it.

Ginny

(*Teasing.*) No, please, please, let me.

Neil

Right-O, then. Jolly good.

Thad

(*Calls out from the front room.*) What time is it? (*Pause. Neil and Ginny return to the living room with tea mugs in hand.*) That's the first time I've thought of the time tonight. (*Ginny sits in the easy chair. Neil squats on the couch. Thad shuffles over to the piano bench, sits down and faces the other two.*)

Neil

(*Playfully.*) Are you gonna say, "I gotta go to bed?"

Thad

No! (*Defensive.*)

Neil

No way. No way!

Thad

Have you thought of time yet?

Neil

Me? No.

Thad

(Talking to himself.) This is the first time I thought of time. *(Speaking to Neil and Ginny.)* So, I just wondered what time it was.

Ginny

(Wants Thad to guess the time.) About what time is it?

Thad

That's the point!

Neil

(Looks at watch.) Oh, it's early. It's only 9:00 p.m.

Thad

Does that have any meaning for us right now?

Neil

Yeah ... yeah, on one level it does. To me, it means it's not too late. It's not very late. *(Thad cracks up.)*

Ginny

(Playfully banters with Neil. It's a comedy routine.) I knew he'd find that funny. That is kind of funny though.

Neil

What's kind of funny?

Ginny

That is kind of funny.

Neil

Oh, that it's not too late?

Ginny

Yeah.

Thad

(Smiles big.) This is great!

Neil

Why is that not so funny? *(Looks at Ginny.)*

Ginny

No, it is kind of funny.

Neil

Oh! Why is that funny?

Ginny

I don't know. I mean, I thought that's funny in a minor way and I knew he'd find it funny in a major way. But, I don't really know why it's funny either.

Thad

That's far out!

Neil

(Looks at Ginny. Imitates Groucho Marx's voice and the comic's well-known cigar routine.) And he had less than I had.

Ginny

But he weighs less. *(Replies with same Marx gesture and voice.)*

Thad

(Answers with the Marx imitation.) I weigh less.

Neil

(Replies in the same manner.) That's right. He weighs less. That's right. *(Drops the Marx imitation. Long pause. Stands, walks to the middle of the room and clears his throat.)*

Thad

Go for it!

Neil

Part of sitting in a Quaker silent meeting for an hour; you know, a Friends Meeting, is that thing we were talking about earlier. But an hour, it's just like touching the surface. Just touching on it.

Thad

That's right.

Neil

However, everybody at that meeting understands.

Thad

Knows that.

Ginny

(Playful kidding.) Knows what?

Neil

Knows that!

Thad

Right!

Neil

And … shit … what an interesting assortment of people at that Quaker Meeting wherever it is, you know. And it's like what led all of us to that?

Ginny

That is wild!

Neil

Just like last year. When I was attending mass … you know … at St. Andrew's Church. *(Pause.)* I forget the ritual. *(Pause.)* Whew, I'm goin' now. I am really goin'! *(Everyone's laughing.)* You know, the ceremony where you get up, stand in a line and kiss the feet of Christ.

Thad

Yeah.

Neil

(With excitement like in a game of Charades.) It's on, uh? What is that? Is that part of Easter?

Thad

No!

Neil

Can we … can we pinpoint that? Where is that? *(Looks at Ginny.)*

Ginny

(Excited.) Last Supper!

Neil

No, no, no, no, no, it has nothing to do with the Last … *(Points to Thad.)*

Ginny

(Insistent.) Yeah, Last Supper!

Thad

No, it's Good Friday!

Ginny

Good Friday?

Neil

Oh! And is that where they … where everybody lines up and kisses his feet? *(Sits down at the desk facing the other two.)*

Thad

Sure! I'm right! He's dead!

Neil

(Leans into telling his story.) Well, you see, the first time I witnessed that ritual, I wouldn't do that. I would not kiss his feet! I just held back. *(Chuckles.)* Somehow, I'm gonna tie this into the conversation.

Thad

Keep going. Keep going. This is far out.

Neil

Okay. *(Draws out the story.)* I wouldn't do that. And I didn't even begin to appreciate what that was all about. And then the second go around ... this past year ... there was no problem kissing his feet! No problem at all, you know? I mean it was like ... *(Laughs at himself. Looks back and forth at Thad and Ginny.)* Are you there? Are you here? Are you with me?

Thad

Yeah!

Ginny

Yeah, we're with you.

Neil

Okay. It's like sitting at the ...

Thad

I'm in a lot of other places, too. *(Pause.)* You know it's all together!

Neil

Yeah! It's like sitting at the Quaker Meeting and all the assortment of people here and how we all came to the common understanding of the importance of this. And also it's like being there in the cathedral kissing the feet of Christ with a line of seventy-five other people. *(Laughs again. Amazed at what's un-*

folding in his imagination.) And, it's like being there sitting Buddhist meditation in the temple. And it's like, it's like ... Isn't that interesting how we all came to the community of that. I mean ... I mean ... *(Revelation.)* It really is all the same thing, ya know!

All

Right! *(High five one another. Pause.)*

Neil

It's all rooted back here in our *silent meeting,* like tonight. *(Pats his right hand against his heart.)* I think that's where the roots are really. *(Pause.)*

Thad

(Eyes closed.) Yeah, *cultivate the quiet garden.* That's what always comes back to me.

Ginny

Right. That's right. That's right.

Thad

It's like a remembrance; a memorial. *Cultivate the quiet garden* is the memorial.

All

(Slowly and quietly chant.) Cultivate the quiet garden. Cultivate the quiet garden. Cultivate the quiet garden … (Pause.)

Ginny

'Cause there are links. There are many links.

Thad

All the time, you know. That's what's so funny.

Neil

(Jumps up.) All the time! *(Moves about the room speaking, rhythmically, like a holy roller preacher.)* That's right! That's right …

Thad

(Jumps up with Ginny and they begin to move around, too, talking the preacher talk. All three play off one another.) See, it's like no big deal, you know! We go into all this labor …

Ginny

All this labor … we go into all this labor!

Neil

(Keeps up the rhythm in a humorous and serious manner). Fighting it! I mean like all our lives. Like ... Arrgh! ... me! I know that inside. I know it! So ... and then when it's so simple to just let it down! And it's right there all along! And it's sort of like ...

Ginny

There are sooo many levels!

Neil

(Maintains the preacher rhythm.) There are sooo many levels! Oh yea, so many levels! But, but I do think. I think right now! That it comes down to letting it all go!

All

Let it go! Let it go! Let it go ...

Neil

And that feels good ... God! *(Hands stretched out looking upwards.)* I feel great! Things will change!

Thad

Feels good … God! I feel great, too! Things will change!

Ginny

That's right! That's right! Things will change! Amen!

Neil

Things are changing! *(Pause. Drops the preacher talk.)* Maybe that'll become my grandfather's Navajo rug. Right? *(Neil, Ginny and Thad look at one another, laugh and shrug their shoulders.)*

Thad

Oh, wow. Wow! *(Thad and Ginny return to the couch.)*

Neil

(Laughing.) In fact, in a way, it seemed to have become that, you know? *(Moves to the easy chair.)* 'Cause there's always reference back there somewhere. And, it's made sense.

Ginny

(Teasing.) In a manner of speaking.

Neil

No, not even in a manner of speaking. *(Defensive.)* It makes sense. It made sense. No qualifiers are required. It made sense.

Ginny

(Razzing.) Of course! *(Pause.)*

Neil

(Stands up and almost stumbles.) Oops! *(Steadies himself and starts to head towards the kitchen.)* One foot there … and the other foot there. *(Laughs at himself.)*

Thad

Can I play the piano again and see what that feels like? *(Wanders over to the piano and sits down.)*

Ginny

Sure, sweetheart.

Neil

(*Laughing.*) I'm up walking. You can play the piano now. (*Meanders over to the piano and leans up against it.*)

Thad

(*Plays a few chords, stops and turns around.*) If I could put that line into a song … (*Sings slowly with a country western twang.*) *Cultivate your quiet gardens. Oh, cultivate your quiet gardens. Yeah, cultivate your quiet gardens* … (*Neil and Ginny hum the melody briefly. Pause.*) It's performing, see!

Neil

Yeah and sometimes … and I was feeling that.

Ginny

And we were all getting into that preacher act.

Neil

Yeah, we were getting into it. And there's … there's …

Thad

There's nothing left to do but to perform this wild … this thing that's happening which is life. It's like when I was playing before? *(Pause.)* It was fun to have a body. But it was like I was ... outside of it. I was ... uh... It was like I was ... And it was just so amazing! *(Swings back around, plays a few notes then turns back around.)*

Neil

That process ...

Thad

To be alive!

Ginny

Oh yeah, being alive!

Thad

And that's all we're basically saying, over and over again.

Neil

(Pause.) That's true.

Ginny

Well it ... varies, too, because ... because ...

Thad

It does vary.

Ginny

(Completes her thought.) because in our preacher performance, I couldn't quite find the words. *(Pause.)* Like the words were sort of not the point. *(Laughs.)* And I'm not tripping either!

Thad

That's what I'm laughing about half the time, too. Yeah.

Ginny

(Addresses Neil who is still leaning against the piano.) But what you were saying before, when you were trying to communicate to me about the silent retreat experience?

Neil

Uh-huh.

Ginny

I was very caught up in the words because there was a point to it other than a performance. But when we were all doing the preacher act, just now, the performance was the point.

(Neil returns to the couch and sits down.)

Ginny

And I was not paying very much attention to the words at all.

Neil

You were with the performance?

Ginny

I was with you and Thad, yeah, the performers and the performance ... the emotions ... the feelings. *(Pause.)* And the words weren't really as important.

Thad

And yet the words are the performance, too.

Ginny

Yeah, I know, but it was the freedom to perform that I was most ...

Thad

Right! That's a whole 'nother great thing.

Ginny

(Completes sentence.) that I was most interested in.

Thad

(Laughing.) Wow!

Ginny

So then, we switched sides. So, that I was not in the word catch; in the word camp.

Neil

That's right. See? *(Long pause.)*

Thad

(Swings around and plays two alternating high notes. Addresses Neil.) Can you narrate?

Neil

What?

Thad

Like, can you narrate what these sounds do to you? *(Continues to play the two notes.)* Can you put it into words for the tape recorder?

Neil

(Speaks with confidence.) Well … if you'll just give me a second, I can. I can do it for you. *(Slowly walks over to the desk and stands by the tape recorder.)*

Thad

Right! Right. *(Piano high notes continue to alternate.)*

Neil

(Long pause. Looks dumbfounded.) Nah … maybe I can't. *(All laughing.)* I don't know! *(Returns to couch and sits down.)*

Thad

And why? Because it keeps changing! *(Plays alternating notes one octave lower than before.)*

Neil

Ah! Right! *(Pause.)* No, but each of those notes does have an effect. That doesn't change.

Thad

The effect doesn't change but the changes keep changing. *(Chokes in high pitched laughter. Scratches the top of his head like a monkey.)* Yes?

Neil

Well that's, that's ... *(Chuckles and shakes his head.)* that's sort of like your damn plaid shirt again. Only it's even more so.

Thad

Anyway ... *(Thad stops playing.)* See, we just started trying to do a simple thing. Can we agree that this is a simple thing that we're trying to do which is like hearing sound and describing it?

Ginny

Now when you start describing ... *(Thad laughs at her.)* No, when you start putting words to it instead of just being ... Arrgh! ... See? *(Thad plays a single note to the beat of a second on a clock.)* But it's all okay. *(Says reassuringly.)*

All

(Chant quietly.) It's all okay. It's all okay. It's all okay ...

Neil

Using words now ... that will have an effect ... *(Gives up. Can't make sense of what he's saying.)* I feel redundant! You know, it's like ... *(Pause.)* You know, there's night ... and day.

Ginny

But that's the beauty of it.

Neil

The redundancy?

Thad

Yes, it's the same beautiful message over and over again in different ways. And so part of us ... It feels like it's a drag because it is redundant. *(Moves to the couch.)*

Ginny

It is the same beautiful message over and over again. I like redundancy like that.

Neil

(Doesn't quite get it.) I know.

Thad

It's redundant because it's eternal! *(Slaps his knee.)*

Neil

(Almost gets it.) I think ... I know.

Thad

And it's so far out. It's eternal!

Neil

(Pause.) I know. *(Throws his arms up in the air.)* Now, I know!

Ginny

We all do, don't we!

(Neil, Ginny, and Thad hold hands, lean back into the couch and close their eyes. Immediate blackout except for a single spotlight focused on the end of the recording tape flapping in the air. Pause. Spotlight slowly fades out.)

About the Playwright

William Claassen, former New York actor and member of the Actors' Equity Association, Screen Actors Guild and the American Federation of Radio and Television Artists, performed in Manhattan in the 1970s and early 1980s. He studied with Austin Pendleton at the Herbert Bergoff Studios, Kim Stanley at the Shelter West Theater and Rae Allen, Judith Greentree, Mark Zeller and Dana Zeller at the 78th Street Theater Lab.

Some of Claassen's roles included Ben in *Margaret's Bed* by William Inge, Trofimov in Anton Chekhov's *The Cherry Orchard*, the Sheriff in Stephen Black's *The Pokey*, Ted in Peter Schaffer's *The Private Ear* and the Commentator in Brian Friel's *Lovers*. He was also cast as Joe in William Saroyan's *The Time of Your Life*, Eric in George Blumberg's *Knitters in the Sun* and Mark in Michael Cristofer's *The Shadow Box*.